Young Jim Thorpe

All-American Athlete

A Troll First-Start® Biography

by Edward Farrell
illustrated by Marie DeJohn

Troll Associates

This edition published in 2002.

Library of Congress Cataloging-in-Publication Data

Farrell, Edward, (date)
    Young Jim Thorpe: All-American athlete / by Edward Farrell;
illustrated by Marie DeJohn.
       p.   cm.— (A Troll first-start biography)
    Summary: A brief biography of the American Indian who became known
as one of the greatest all-around athletes of the twentieth century.
      ISBN 0-8167-3764-9 (lib. bdg.)   ISBN 0-8167-3765-7 (pbk.)
    1. Thorpe, Jim, 1888-1953—Juvenile literature.   2. Athletes—
United States—Biography—Juvenile literature.   [1. Thorpe, Jim,
1888-1953.   2. Athletes.   3. Indians of North America—Biography.]
I. DeJohn, Marie, ill.   II. Title.   III. Series.
GV697.T5F37   1996
796'.092—dc20
  [B]   95-10022

Copyright © 1996 by Troll Communications L.L.C.

Published by Troll Associates, an imprint and registered trademark of Troll Communications L.L.C.

All rights reserved. No part of this book may be reproduced or utilized in any form or by any means, electronic or mechanical, including photocopying, recording, or by any information storage and retrieval system, without written permission from the publisher.

Printed in the United States of America.

10 9 8 7 6 5 4 3

Jim Thorpe was one of the greatest athletes of all time.

James Francis Thorpe and his twin brother, Charles, were born on May 28, 1888, on a ranch near Shawnee, Oklahoma.

Their parents, Charlotte and Hiram Thorpe, were members of the Sac and Fox tribes. Charlotte Thorpe was a great-granddaughter of the great Sac chief, Black Hawk.

Life was hard for the Thorpes. They lived on a ranch on an Indian reservation. Mr. Thorpe farmed and hunted. Sometimes he tamed wild horses for extra money.

At home, Jim and Charlie were always playing together. They spoke the Sac and Fox language, just like their parents did.

When the twins were 3, Mr. Thorpe taught them how to ride bareback on a pony. He also taught them how to shoot with a bow and arrow.

Jim and Charlie also loved having races by the barn. Jim could run very fast.

When the twins were 6 years old, they left home to go to a boarding school 23 miles away.

All the students at school had to learn English, so they would fit in with the world outside the reservation.

Jim wasn't a very good student. On the playground, however, he was unbeatable! He was the fastest runner, the longest jumper, and the best hitter in baseball.

Jim and Charlie loved coming home to the ranch during summer vacation. But in the summer after their second year at school, Charlie caught pneumonia and became very sick.

Jim stayed with his brother every day, feeding him and trying to help him get better. But Charlie died later that summer, and Jim became very quiet and sad.

When Jim went back to school, he missed Charlie more than ever. One day he was so lonely and unhappy, he left school and walked the 23 miles back home.

Jim's parents told him he had to go back to school. Jim had to have an education.

The next year Jim left school and walked home again. His parents decided to send him to a school far away, where he couldn't walk home.

Jim's new school was the Haskell Institute, in Lawrence, Kansas. At Haskell, he liked to watch the football team practice every day.

He especially liked to watch Chauncey,
the star of the team.

Chauncey noticed Jim watching and asked him if he wanted to learn how to play. Jim was thrilled. He loved football and was happy to have made a friend.

When Jim was 12, his mother died. Jim asked his father if he could stay home from school and help around the ranch. Mr. Thorpe said yes.

Jim worked hard on the ranch. Then, in the fall of 1904, Jim went to the Carlisle Indian School in Pennsylvania to learn a trade. Carlisle had many good coaches and teams.

Jim was too small to play on the football team, but he practiced and worked out all the time. Finally, in the fall of 1907, Jim made the varsity football team. He was a star from the very first game.

In the spring, Jim ran on the track team and played on the baseball team. Twice he was chosen a football All-American.

In the summer of 1912, Jim went to the Olympics as a member of the U.S. team. He won gold medals in the pentathlon and the decathlon! These events test a person's skills in running, jumping, and throwing.

Then, a few months later, Jim's medals were taken away from him. Olympic athletes were supposed to be unpaid amateurs. Jim had earned a small amount of money playing baseball in 1909.

In 1982, the Olympic Committee decided Jim really deserved the medals. It gave the medals back to Jim's family.

After the Olympics, Jim played major league baseball and professional football.

In 1920, Thorpe became the first president of the American Professional Football Association, which later became the National Football League.

In 1950, three years before he died, Jim Thorpe was voted the greatest athlete of the first half of the twentieth century.